"This is an incredible book. Passionate, informative, and beautifully written, it captures the culture and struggles of Palestine in a brutally realistic yet uplifting way. It is evident that the author approached this work from a place of deep respect and appreciation for the Palestinian culture, a desire to educate others about the struggles experienced by Palestinian people, and a willingness to share this information with the world. In this book, each letter of the alphabet has an associated brief chapter describing a core aspect, symbol, or important event related to Palestine. The author has concisely captured a lot of information and relayed this in a simple and fluid format, which is easy to understand even for those with little prior knowledge such as myself. While the content itself is at times difficult to hear, the author has taken care to emphasise the hope, joy, and perseverance of the Palestinian people, who are still striving for a better future despite having experienced so much adversity. This is a really important and beneficial read for anyone wanting to learn more about the people and culture of Palestine, especially timely nowadays in light of the 2023 Israel-Hamas conflict. I highly recommend this book and cannot give it enough praise."

— Diana Meirinho Domingues,

University of Edinburgh

An ABC of
Palestine

A Journey To Discover Palestine
& the Palestinian People

For Kids & Grown Ups

by Mourad Diouri

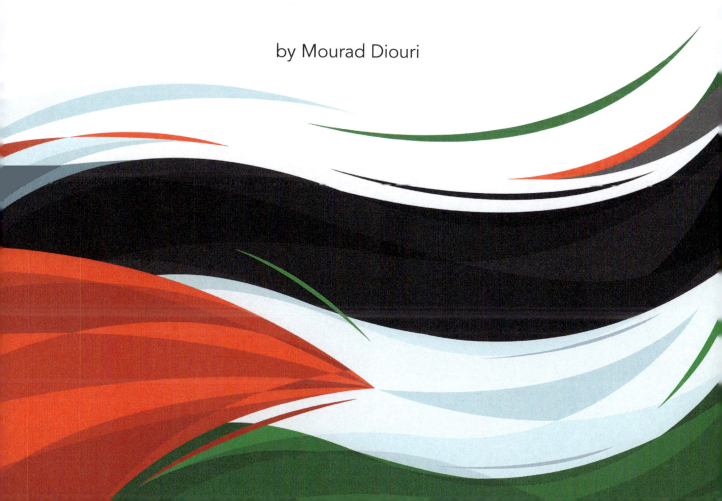

In the name of God, the Most Gracious, the Most Merciful

Key to Visual Icons

🇵🇸	Arabic		🇯🇵	Japanese
🇧🇩	Bengali		🇨🇳	Mandarin Chinese
🇳🇱	Dutch		🇵🇱	Polish
☬	Farsi		🇵🇹	Portuguese
🇫🇷	French		🇷🇺	Russian
🇩🇪	German		🇪🇸	Spanish
🇮🇳	Hindi		🇹🇷	Turkish
🇮🇹	Italian		🇵🇰	Urdu

ISBN 978-1-916524-35-4

The visual icons and illustrations in this book were designed and licensed by freepik.com and flaticon.com
The image of Kufiyyah in 'K' for "Kufiyyah" is by Andrey Atanov via GettyImages

First printing, 2023

Published by Mosaic Tree Press
Browse our complete catalogue of publications at MosaicTree.org

Published by
Mosaic Tree Press

Contents

Dedication 7

Introduction 8

An Abc of Palestine 9

A — is for — Apartheid 10

B — is for — Boycott 12

C — is for — Christianity 14

D — is for — Displacement & Diaspora 16

E — is for — Exile & Eviction 18

F — is for — Freedom 20

G — is for — Gaza (غزة) 22

H — is for — Human Rights 24

I — is for — Islam 28

J — is for — Judaism 30

K — is for — Kufiyyah (كوفية) 32

L — is for — The Right of Land 34

M — is for — Massacres 36

N — is for — Nakba (النكبة) 38

O — is for — Occupation (Colonialism) 40

P — is for — Palestine (فلسطين) 42

Q — is for — Al-Quds (القدس) (Jerusalem) 44

R — is for — Right of Return 48

S — is for — International Solidarity 50

T — is for — Thawra (ثورة) (Revolution) 52

U — is for — Uprising (Intifada) (انتفاضة) 54

V — is for — Victory Sign 56

W — is for — West Bank (الضفة الغربية) 58

X — is for — Xenophobia 60

Y — is for — Yearning for Dignity 64

Z — is for — Zionism 66

An ABC of Solidarity with Palestine: An A-Z Guide to Advocacy and Action 69

Acknowledgments & Final Words 74

Dedication

This book is dedicated to all the resilient people of Palestine, whether residing in your occupied homeland or in the diaspora still searching for peace and justice. This book is a humble tribute to your strength, courage, and enduring spirit as well as to all those who stand in solidarity with Palestine. May it, in its modest capacity, contribute to raising awareness and understanding. May each letter of the alphabet in this book serve as a conversation starter, shedding light on Palestine and the intricacies of the Palestinian issue. In solidarity with all Palestinians and hope for a future marked by peace, freedom, and justice. May God Almighty strengthen you in the face of injustice. You have inspired us all with your strength, courage and hope.

Introduction

"An ABC of Palestine" is an enlightening alphabetical journey through the heart and soul of Palestine, unveiling its rich history, vibrant culture, resilient people, and their enduring struggle against the seventy-five-year-old long Israeli occupation. Each letter of the alphabet uncovers a poignant aspect of the Palestinian experience, from 'A' for Apartheid and 'N' for Nakba, to 'Z' for Zionism.

In this meticulously crafted book, readers will delve into the complexities of Palestine's past and present, exploring topics such as 'B' for Boycotting, highlighting the global efforts to support the Palestinian cause, and 'G' for Gaza, shedding light on the daily struggle faced by its inhabitants. The book also delves into the cultural and religious tapestry of the region, including 'C' for Christianity, 'I' for Islam, and 'J' for Judaism, showcasing the diversity that defines Palestine. Through the pages of "An ABC of Palestine," readers will confront the harsh realities of displacement, exile, and eviction ('D' for Displacement & Diaspora, 'E' for Exile & Eviction), and the resilience of a people determined to reclaim their homeland, as depicted in 'R' for Right of Return and 'T' for Thawra (Revolution). The book also sheds light on the unwavering spirit of the Palestinian people, their commitment to human rights ('H' for Human Rights), and the global solidarity efforts ('S' for International Solidarity) that have emerged in support of their struggle.

With captivating illustrations and poignant narratives, "An ABC of Palestine" serves as a crucial tool for raising awareness, fostering understanding, and inspiring change. It encourages readers to unite in solidarity with the Palestinian people, recognising their unwavering longing for dignity ('Y' for Yearning for Dignity) and steadfast resistance against Xenophobia ('X' for Xenophobia).

This book is not just an alphabet primer; it is a testament to the indomitable spirit of a nation, a call for justice, and a tribute to the enduring legacy of Palestine.

This book aims to raise awareness, challenge misconceptions, and ignite meaningful conversations in an easily understandable manner about the complex and pressing issue of Palestine and the Palestinian struggle. Designed to be both child-friendly and accessible to adults, it aims to foster inter-generational dialogues to help shed light on the issues.

Every purchase contributes directly to humanitarian and medical aid in Palestine, as 100% of the proceeds from the sale of this book are dedicated to supporting those in need. By delving into the heart of the matter, I hope this book will inspire empathy, understanding, and tangible support for a cause that demands our attention and solidarity.

	A	is for	Apartheid		**N**	is for	Nakba (النكبة)
	B	is for	Boycott		**O**	is for	Occupation (Colonialism)
	C	is for	Christianity		**P**	is for	Palestine (فلسطين)
	D	is for	Displacement & Diaspora		**Q**	is for	Al-Quds (القدس) (Jerusalem)
	E	is for	Exile & Eviction		**R**	is for	Right of Return
	F	is for	Freedom		**S**	is for	International Solidarity
	G	is for	Gaza (غزة)		**T**	is for	Thawra (ثورة) (Revolution)
	H	is for	Human Rights		**U**	is for	Uprising (Intifada انتفاضة)
	I	is for	Islam		**V**	is for	Victory Sign
	J	is for	Judaism		**W**	is for	West Bank (الضفة الغربية)
	K	is for	Kufiyyah (كوفية)		**X**	is for	Xenophobia
	L	is for	The Right of Land		**Y**	is for	Yearning for Dignity
	M	is for	Massacres		**Z**	is for	Zionism

A

is for

Apartheid

فصل عنصري

আপার্টহাইট

Apartheid

آپارتاید (آنتی‌نژادپارتی)

Apartheid

Apartheid

श्वेतवाद

Apartheid

アパルトヘイト

种族隔离制度

Apartheid

Apartheid

Апартеид

Apartheid

Irksal ayrımcılık

اپارتھائیڈ

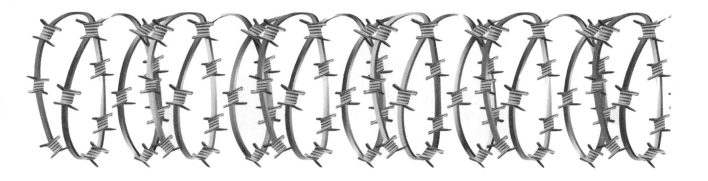

Imagine a world where people are separated and treated unfairly because of who they are. That's **apartheid**, and it's a harsh reality for Palestinians under the ongoing Israeli occupation. Just like the people of South Africa who fought against apartheid, Palestinians face unjust laws and divisions, reminiscent of a painful history. But amid this struggle, they display incredible strength, uniting against inequality. Resisting **apartheid** symbolises their determination for equality, highlighting a collective spirit that refuses to be broken. **Apartheid** signifies separate rules and opportunities for different groups, breeding inequality. One notable instance of **apartheid** in Palestine is the **Separation Apartheid Barrier/Wall** or the Security Fence (according to Israelis), which stands as a glaring symbol of apartheid, marking segregated zones, restricting movement, and perpetuating systemic discrimination. Its existence mirrors historical injustices, echoing the **apartheid** era in South Africa and reminding the world of the ongoing struggle for equality and human rights in Palestine. The Palestinian struggle against this oppression epitomises their fight for dignity, freedom, and self-determination, capturing the world's attention and compassion.

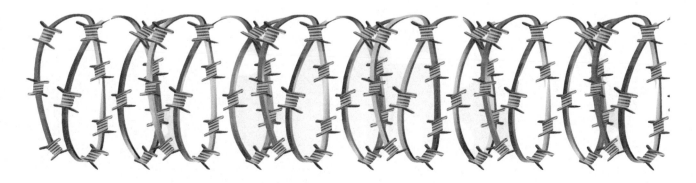

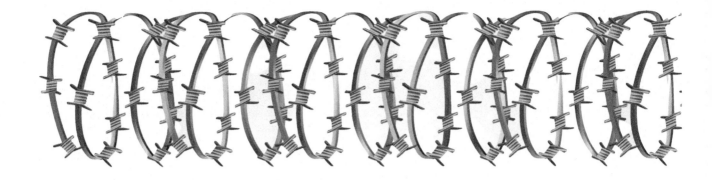

Due to the Israeli imposed blockade on the Gaza strip, virtually isolating it completely from the outside world, Palestinians in Gaza have experienced **quarantine-like conditions,** affecting their ability to trade, travel, and live normal lives:

(1) Restricted Movement: Gazans face severe restrictions on movement, both within the territory and to the outside world. The blockade has limited their ability to travel for education, work, and medical treatment. This is achieved by the closure of borders with Palestine as well as military checkpoints to and from Gaza.

(2) Economic Strain: The blockade has crippled Gaza's economy. Restrictions on imports and exports have led to high unemployment rates and a lack of essential goods and resources.

(3) Humanitarian Crisis: The blockade has contributed to a mounting humanitarian crisis in Gaza. Limited access to clean water, electricity, and healthcare services has created dire living conditions for its 2.2 million residents.

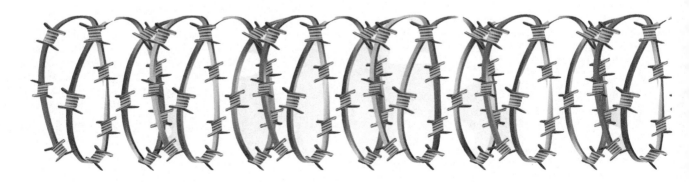

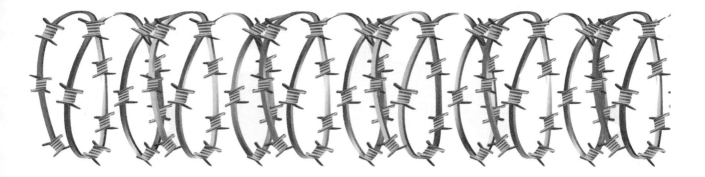

(4) Impact on Education: Students in Gaza struggle to access quality education due a shortage of resources and restricted movement hinder their ability to attend schools and universities regularly.

(5) Healthcare Challenges: The healthcare system in Gaza is crippled. Medical supplies and equipment are scarce, making it difficult to provide adequate care to patients. Travel restrictions also hinder patients from seeking specialised treatment outside Gaza.

(6) Psychological Impact: The prolonged blockade has taken a toll on the mental health of Gaza's residents. Living in isolation, with limited opportunities and resources, has led to widespread despair and frustration among the population.

(7) Generational Impact: For the younger generation in Gaza, the blockade has been a constant reality, some children never knowing life without it. Children and young adults have grown up in an environment of limited opportunities, affecting their education, aspirations, and overall well-being. It has been reported that 80% of Gaza children suffer depression after 15 years of blockade as 800,000 children in Gaza have only ever known life under blockade, affecting their mental health [1]

[1] "Trapped" report, by Save the Children, (2022) (Source: https://bit.ly/3G2jXkl)

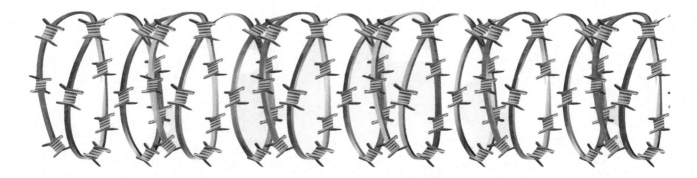

B

is for

Boycott

مقاطعة

বয়কট

Boycotting

بویکات (تحریم)

Boycott

Boykott

बहिष्कार

Boicottaggio

ボイコット

集体抵制

Bojkotowanie

Boicote

Бойкотирование

Boicot

Boykot

بائیکاٹ کرنا

14

Boycott is a powerful form of protest, a peaceful weapon employed against injustices. It is not entirely restricted to refusing to buy products or support businesses linked to the funding of Israel, but also expands to cultural and educational realms; echoing the frustration of Palestinians with Israeli policies. This act, akin to not engaging with someone who isn't being fair, represents a non-violent channel for expression, where wallets become voices and choices become statements. **Boycotting** helps Palestinians reclaim a sense of control, standing united against what they perceive an oppressive power. It's part of a larger effort to raise global awareness, rallying individuals and nations to empathise with the Palestinian cause. Through this grassroots movement, Palestinians hope to promote change, fostering a world where justice and fairness prevail over oppression. The most prominent boycott movement related to Israel is the **BDS (Boycott, Divestment and Sanctions)** movement, an international Palestinian-led movement promoting boycotts, divestments, and economic sanctions against Israel throughout the world.

C

is for

Christianity

المسيحية

খ্রিষ্টধর্ম

Christendom

مسیحیت

Christianisme

Christentum

ईसाई धर्म

Cristianesimo

キリスト教

基督教

Chrześcijaństwo

Cristianismo

Христианство

Cristianismo

Hristiyanlık

عیسائیت

Christianity in Palestine refers to the presence and practice of the Christian faith in the region, where Jesus Christ was born over 2,000 years ago. Many important religious sites, like **Bethlehem (بيت لحم)** and **Jerusalem (القدس)**, are in Palestine, making it a deeply significant and holy place for **Christians** worldwide. However, the reality for **Christian Palestinians** living in the occupied territories is marked by oppression under Israeli occupation, which includes the targeting of their places of worship. **Christians** in Palestine follow the teachings of Jesus and celebrate traditions like **Christmas** and **Easter**, playing a vital role in the cultural fabric of Palestine alongside the Muslim and Jewish communities. It's crucial to recognise that not all Palestinians who live in Palestine are Muslims; **Christian Palestinians** contribute significantly to the rich religious diversity of the region, emphasising the importance of peaceful coexistence and understanding among different faiths. **Christian Palestinians** continue to stand united with their Muslim compatriots, jointly striving for freedom against the continued Israeli occupation. Recent data indicates that Gaza is home to a diminishing population of 800-1000 **Palestinian Christians**, representing the world's oldest Christian community dating back to the first century. This historic community faces a grave threat of ethnic cleansing as a result of the recent Israeli bombardments in 2023.[1]

[1] See "Gaza's Christians fear 'threat of extinction' amid Israel war" by Aljazeera.com (bit.ly/3sJ35vW) [10 Nov 2023]

D

is for

Displacement &
Diaspora

التهجير والشتتات

উত্পাটন এবং বিক্ষিপ্ত উদ্বাসন

Verplaatsing en Diaspora

جا به جا شدگی/ جوامع دور از وطن

Déplacement et Diaspora

Vertreibung und Diaspora

विस्थापन और प्रवास

Dislocamento e Diaspora

強制移住とディアスポラ

强制迁移和流散

Przesiedlenie i diaspora

Deslocamento e Diáspora

Вытеснение и Диаспора

Desplazamiento y Diáspora

Zorunlu Göç ve Diaspora

ہجرت اور دیاسپورا

Displacement for Palestinians means being forced from their home and removed from their own land. Imagine leaving everything behind - your possessions, your home, your memories and your history. Many Palestinians are facing that reality, their families were uprooted and are living far away from their homeland. It's like having a piece of your heart in a place you can't reach. Despite this pain, Palestinians carry their heritage, like stars in the night sky, connecting them across far distances. Since the establishment of Israel in 1948, many Palestinians have experienced numerous **displacements**, leading to the loss of their homes, communities, and way of life. This **displacement**, known in Arabic as **the Nakba** (i.e. "the catastrophe"), continues to impact generations upon generations of Palestinians, creating a deep sense of loss and a longing of return to their homeland. **Displacement** has resulted in the formation of refugee camps and communities in different parts of the world, marking a significant aspect of the Palestinian struggle for justice and the **right to return** [1] to their ancestral lands. Palestinian refugees live in around 68 Palestinian refugee camps across Jordan, Lebanon, Syria, Egypt, the West Bank and the Gaza Strip, as well as globally around the world.

[1] See 'R' for "Right of Return"

الطرد والنفى 🇵🇸

নির্বাসন এবং উচ্ছেদ 🇧🇩

Ballingschap en Uitzetting 🇳🇱

تبعيد و اخراج ☬

Exil et Expulsion 🇫🇷

Exil und Zwangsräumung 🇩🇪

निर्वासन और निकालापन 🇮🇳

Esilio ed Espulsione 🇮🇹

国外追放と強制退去 🇯🇵

流亡与驱逐 🇨🇳

Wygnanie i wysiedlenie

The tale of **Palestinian exile and eviction** is a saddening narrative etched in history, marked by forced displacement, occupation, and unwavering resilience. More than 6 million Palestinians, accounting for one of the world's largest and oldest refugee populations, live scattered across the globe due to the Israeli occupation [1] , and by 2023, 5.9 million people were registered as eligible for UNRWA [2] services (in 59 recognised refugee camps in Jordan, Lebanon, Syria, the West Bank, and the Gaza Strip). These individuals, rooted in generations of heritage, carry the essence of Palestine within them, fostering a tenacious spirit despite the daily struggle they face. Their homes, once brimming with cherished memories, now echo with the haunting remnants of displacement and resilience. Despite adversity, **Palestinians in exile** preserve their cultural heritage, passing down traditions and stories, ensuring Palestine's legacy endures. Through vibrant global communities, they contribute significantly to various fields, while grassroots organisations advocate for their right to return and raise awareness about ongoing struggles. The hope for a homeland persists.

[1] "The Palestinian Diaspora: Global Exchange" (2013/01/01)
[2] UNRWA: The United Nations Relief and Works Agency for Palestine Refugees in the Near East.

F

is for

Freedom

حرية

স্বাধীনতা

Vrijheid

آزادی

Liberté

Freiheit

स्वतंत्रता

Libertà

自由

自由

Wolności i prawa

Liberdade

Свобода

Libertad

Özgürlük

آزادی

In the context of Palestine, **freedom** embodies the fundamental aspiration for peace, existence, and the power to shape their own destiny. Living within the confines of Israeli occupation, these fundamental liberties are constrained, emerging as central objectives in the Palestinian quest for freedom. Imagine a life where you cannot move freely, where your everyday choices are constrained. Palestinians, whether residing in occupied territories or scattered in diaspora, encounter these challenges daily; nevertheless, their resilience remains unbroken. Their resilience shines through as they persistently fight for these basic rights, hoping for a future where they can live in peace, decide their own fate, and move without limitations. In the midst of this struggle, **the dove** stand as a powerful symbol of peace and **freedom in Palestine**. Just as Palestinians long for freedom, these gentle birds represent their enduring hope for peace and dignity. [1]

[1] See 'H' for "Human Rights" for a detailed list of human rights violations.

G

is for

Gaza
غزة

غزة

গাজা ভূখণ্ড

Gaza

غزه

Gaza

Gaza

गज़ा (Gazā)

Gaza

ガザ

加沙

Gaza

Gaza

Газа

Gaza

Gazze

غزہ

Gaza, a narrow coastal strip in Palestine [1], symbolises immense resilience amid adversity. Home to nearly 2.2 million people, it grapples with severe challenges imposed by strict border controls, limiting access to fundamental necessities like clean water, electricity and healthcare. Often dubbed the world's largest **open-air prison**, Gaza's inhabitants endure these restrictions with resolute courage, embodying the unyielding spirit of Palestinians. In **Gaza**, Palestinians withstand recurring violence, suffering from ongoing killings and oppression perpetrated by the Israeli military. The devastating impact of this brutality became apparent during the latest wave of aggression in 2023, resulting in more than 13,000 Palestinians losing their lives and over 30,000 sustaining injuries [2]. Among the casualties were 5,500 children with a distressing statistic revealing the loss of one Palestinian child every ten minutes since October 7th, 2023. The majority of those affected were women, children, and the elderly. It is important to note that the number of casualties continues to rise under the continuous bombing of civilians by the Israeli army. Their daily struggle in Gaza has inspired global solidarity calling for freedom and peace for the Palestinians. Despite the harsh conditions, **Gazan people** continue to demonstrate remarkable strength, fortifying the worldwide demand for justice in support of the Palestinian cause.

[1] The Gaza Strip is 41 km (25 miles) long, and from 6-12 km (3.7 to 7.5 mi) wide, and has a total area of 365 km² (141 sq mi).
[2] These figures are based on available data at the time of writing and are subject to change as the situation evolves.

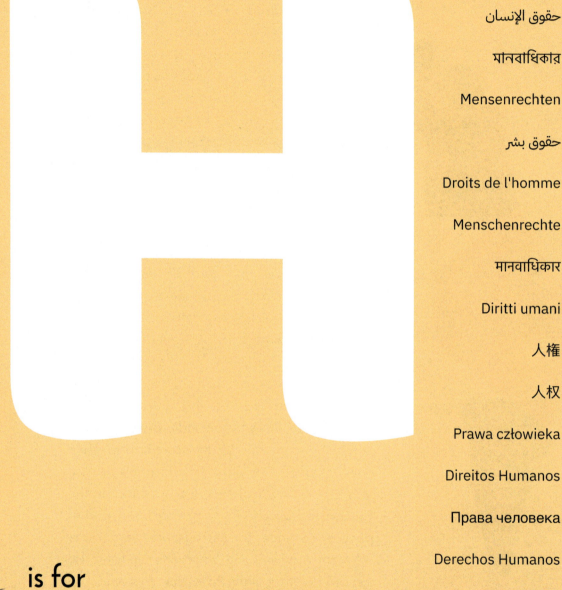

H

is for

Human Rights

حقوق الإنسان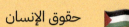

মানবাধিকার

Mensenrechten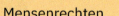

حقوق بشر

Droits de l'homme

Menschenrechte

मानवाधिकार

Diritti umani

人権

人权

Prawa człowieka

Direitos Humanos

Права человека

Derechos Humanos

İnsan Hakları

انسانی حقوق

Under Israeli occupation, Palestinians face several major violations of **human rights**, drawing international concern, criticism and condemnation. These violations include:

(1) **Restrictions of Movement** due to checkpoints, roadblocks, and the separation barrier – not to mention the closure of entire neighbourhoods due to supposed "Military Activity". That may rise to total home confinement which can last for days. These restrictions also impede access to essential services, education, healthcare, and economic opportunities.

(2) **Illegal Settlements** in the occupied territories violate international law, leading to forced displacement of Palestinians, land confiscation, and destruction of property.

(3) **Home Demolitions** are frequent, leaving families homeless and displaced.

(4) **Violence and Harassment:** Palestinians endure ongoing violence and harassment from Israeli forces and settlers. This includes arbitrary arrests, physical abuse, and even illegal killings without a trial or legal process.

(5) **Detention Without Trial:** Palestinians, including children, are often detained without trial under the guise of 'administrative detentions', a practice frequently criticised by human rights organisations.

(6) **Limited Access to Basic Services:** Palestinians in Gaza face a blockade that severely restricts access to food, water, electricity, fuel for transportation and electric generators for hospitals and gas used for cooking and medical supplies, resulting in a humanitarian crisis that persists both during times of conflict and in their day-to-day lives.

(7) Violations of Freedom of Expression: Palestinian and non-Palestinian journalists, activists, and human rights defenders face censorship, arrest, and harassment for their work. Some were killed like Shireen Abu Akleh [1] and Rachel Corrie [1].

(8) Inadequate Access to Education and Healthcare: Palestinian children often face disruptions in their education due to closures, checkpoints, and violence. Access to healthcare is limited, impacting public health.

(9) Water and Resource Discrimination: Palestinians often receive less water and have limited access to natural resources compared to Israeli settlers, leading to disparities in living conditions. This is because Israel is able to control supply lines of these basic needs before they reach Palestine and have the ability to completely cut them off as witnessed in the recent 2023 conflict.

(10) Denial of Right to Self-Determination: Palestinians are denied the right to self-determination, a fundamental principle of international law, impeding their ability to shape their political and economic future. These violations have been documented and criticised by various human rights organisations, United Nations bodies, and advocacy groups.

[1] Shireen Abu Akleh was a prominent Palestinian-American journalist who worked for Al Jazeera, before she was killed by an Israeli soldier while wearing a blue press vest and covering a raid on the Jenin refugee camp in the Israeli-occupied West Bank
[2] 23-year-old peace activist Rachel Corrie is crushed to death by Israeli bulldozer (bit.ly/40Dbei2)

is for

Islam

الإسلام 🇵🇸

ইসলাম 🇧🇩

Islam 🇳🇱

اسلام ☪

Islam 🇫🇷

Islam 🇩🇪

इस्लाम (Islam) 🇮🇳

Islam 🇮🇹

イスラム教 🇯🇵

伊斯兰教 🇨🇳

Islam 🇵🇱

Islã 🇵🇹

Ислам 🇷🇺

Islam 🇪🇸

İslam 🇹🇷

اسلام 🇵🇰

In Palestine, **Islam** is not just a religion; it's a guiding light, the heartbeat of Palestinian Muslims and their enduring spirit under Israeli occupation. The majority of Palestinians are **Muslims**, finding strength in their faith. Islam's teachings of patience, compassion, and unity inspire their resilience. **The Al-Aqsa Mosque** (المسجــد الأقصى) in Jerusalem, one of Islam's holiest sites, stands as a symbol of hope and steadfastness for Palestinians [1]. Despite the occupation, **Muslims in Palestine** gather there to pray, showcasing their single-minded determination. **The Dome of the Rock,** another iconic site, signifies their deep connection to the land. These sacred places unite Palestinians, reminding them of their heritage and the importance of standing together. Palestine holds vital significance in Islam due to the presence of **Al-Aqsa Mosque,** which is linked to a pivotal event in Islamic tradition, known as "The Night Journey of Prophet Muhammad (SAW)" or (Isra and Mi'raj الإسراء والـــعراج), in Arabic. During this miraculous journey, the Prophet was transported from Mecca to Jerusalem, symbolising a profound spiritual ascent through the heavens. This celestial voyage holds immense significance in Islam, highlighting the divine connection between the earthly and heavenly realms, and it is commemorated as a testament to the Prophet's elevated status and closeness to Allah. Visiting Al-Aqsa is deemed virtuous by Palestinians and Muslims globally. Muslims worldwide deeply value the sacred land of Palestine and its significance in Islamic teachings is paramount, uniting believers in a shared reverence for this sacred place.

[1] See more information about Jerusalem under 'Q' for "Al-Quds"

is for

Judaism

اليهودية	🇵🇸
ইহুদি ধর্ম	🇧🇩
Jodendom	🇳🇱
یهودیت	🇮🇷
Judaïsme	🇫🇷
Judentum	🇩🇪
यहूदियत	🇮🇳
Ebraismo	🇮🇹
ユダヤ教	🇯🇵
犹太教	🇨🇳
Judaizm	🇵🇱
Judaísmo	🇵🇹
Иудаизм	🇷🇺
Judaísmo	🇪🇸
Yahudilik	🇹🇷
یہودیت	🇵🇰

Judaism has a rich historical and cultural significance in Palestine. Considered one of the world's oldest monotheistic religions, it has deep roots in the region. Palestinians have a diverse cultural heritage that includes various religious traditions. **Arab Jews**, also known as Mizrahi Jews, have had a historical presence in Palestine that dates back centuries. Before the establishment of the State of Israel in 1948, Jewish communities, including Arab Jews, lived in harmony alongside **Arab Muslims** and **Arab Christians** in various parts of the region. **Arab Jews** shared a cultural and linguistic heritage with their non-Jewish neighbours, contributing to the diverse tapestry of Palestinian society. Guided by Judaism, many Jews across the world stand in solidarity with Palestinians, calling for freedom from occupation, equality, coexistence, human rights and a peaceful resolution. This viewpoint contrasts with Zionism, a political ideology detailed under 'Z' for Zionism. It's important to note that not all Jews adhere to Zionism, and conversely, not all Zionists are Jewish. Many Jews around the world have formed activist groups such as **'Jewish Voices for Peace'** calling for their faith to be distinguished from the ideology of Zionism and actively call for justice for the Palestinians, often reciting the phrase *'Not in our name'*.

is for

Kufiyyah
كوفية

كوفية

কুফিয়া মাফলার

Kufiyyah

كوفيه

Kufiyyah

Kufiyyah

कुफ़िय्याह

Kufiyyah

クーフィーヤ

库菲耶

Kefija

Kufiyyah

Куфия

Kufiyyah

Keffiye 🇹🇷

کُفیہ 🇵🇰

34

The Kufiyyah or **Keffiyeh,** is also known in Arabic as a Ghutrah (غُتْرَة), Shemagh (شَـــماغ), or ḥaṭṭah (حَطَّة). It is a traditional headdress worn by men from parts of the Middle East. The **Kufiyyah**, a cherished Palestinian scarf, transcends its fabric nature, symbolising resistance and unity against oppression. The **Kufiyyah** has become a symbol of Palestinian national pride, dating back to the 1936-1939 Arab revolt in Palestine. Internationally and outside of the Middle East and North Africa, the **Kufiyyah** gained popularity among activists supporting the Palestinian cause and so is an icon of Palestinian solidarity. Worn with pride, it embodies the collective spirit of people confronting occupation, oppression, and injustice. Each fold tells a tale of generations resilient in adversity, connecting Palestinians to their heritage. It signifies pride and commitment to preserving their cultural identity amid trials. The patterns on the **Kufiyyah** are not random nor are they just for their atheistic appeal. The pattern on the **Kuffiyah** represents the 'fishnet' in homage to Palestine's famous fishing industry which remains a lifeline for the besieged Gaza Strip's economy. Furthermore, the lines on the other side of the **Kufiyyah** represent the olive leaf – an enduring symbol of Palestinian authenticity. The **olive tree** [1] is a matter of life and death for Palestinians – it is their national treasure, from the fruits to the oil, many olive trees in Palestine are several hundreds years old, passing from generation to generation.

[1] Read more about the "Olive Tree" under 'L' for "The Right of Land"

L

حق الأرض

জমির অধিকার

Grondrecht

حق سرزمین / حق قلمرو

Droit à la terre

Recht auf Land

भूमि का अधिकार

Diritto alla Terra

土地の権利

土地权

Prawo do ziemi

Direito à Terra

Право на землю

Derecho a la Tierra

Arazi Hakkı

زمین کا حق

is for

The Right of
Land

The Right of Land for Palestinians is a fundamental human right recognised internationally. It signifies their right to live on and cultivate their ancestral lands, a connection deeply rooted in their history and identity. However, this right has been severely violated due to the Israeli occupation. **Illegal Israeli settlements** in the occupied Palestinian land violate international law, including the **Fourth Geneva Convention**. These settlements continue to expand, encroaching on Palestinian land, displacing families, and obstructing peace. The construction of these settlements remains a major obstacle to peace, perpetuating tension and conflict in the region. The international community widely condemns these settlements as breaching International law, considering them a significant barrier to achieving a just and lasting resolution. **The Right of Land** embodies their quest for dignity, echoing through generations. It's a plea for justice, a plea for the world to recognise their pain. **The Right of Land** signifies their unswerving spirit that refuses to be silenced. The fight for their land isn't just a battle for property; it's a universal quest for justice, illustrating the fundamental human right to belong and live in peace on the land they call home. In every **olive tree**, in every stone of their homes, lies the essence of their resilience. **The Olive Tree** is a vital symbol of peace in Palestine, often referred to as the **"Land of Olives."** Christian history in Palestine is intricately connected to the Olive tree. Tradition suggests that Jesus returned from the Mount of Olives, east of the Al-Aqsa Compound and that he left his companions to pray amid the olive trees in the Gethsemane Garden, situated at the base of the Mount of Olives, where he was subsequently arrested by the Romans.

M

مجازر 🇯🇴

গণহত্যা 🇧🇩

Massamoorden 🇳🇱

قتل‌عام‌ها 🇮🇷

Massacres 🇫🇷

Massaker 🇩🇪

नरसंहार 🇮🇳

Massacri 🇮🇹

大量虐殺 🇯🇵

大屠杀 🇨🇳

Masakry 🇱🇻

Massacres 🇵🇹

Массовые убийства 🇷🇺

Masacres 🇪🇸

Katliam 🇹🇷

نرسنہار 🇵🇰

is for

Massacres

The Palestinian people have endured horrific **massacres**, **genocides**, and relentless killings in their homeland, leaving deep wounds in the fabric of their society. Tragically, these acts have claimed innocent lives, shattered families, and scarred communities. The cycle of violence has perpetuated immense suffering, hindering the prospects of peace and stability in the region. Several notable massacres occurred in Palestine, resulting in significant loss of life, namely: **(1) Deir Yassin Massacre (1948):** where over 100 Palestinian villagers were killed by Jewish paramilitary groups. **(2) Sabra and Shatila Massacre (1982):** hundreds to thousands of Palestinian refugees were killed in Lebanese refugee camps by Lebanese Christian militias while Israel controlled the area. **(3) Jenin Massacre (2002):** during the Israeli military operation in the Jenin refugee camp many were killed where the exact number of casualties remains disputed. **(4) Gaza Massacres (2008-2009, 2014, 2023):** thousands of civilian Palestinians were killed resulting in over 2,100 Palestinian deaths (in 2014) and in 2023 over 11,000 Palestinians, half of which were women and children and more than 100 UN relief agency workers were killed. The recent events in Gaza (2023) also witnessed the unprecedented targeted bombings of civilian structures such as hospitals, schools, bakeries and residential homes, leaving hundreds dead and injured. These incidents highlight the devastating toll on Palestinian lives, underlining the urgency for a peaceful resolution to the conflict so that Palestinians can live in dignity and security, free from violence.

N

is for

Nakba (النكبة)
The Palestinian Catastrophe

النكبة

"נאקבא"

De Nakba

نكبت

La Nakba

Die Nakba

द नक्बा

La Nakba

ナクバ

纳克巴(巴勒斯坦灾难日)

Nakba ('katastrofa')

A Nakba

Накба

La Nakba

Nekbe

نكبہ

The Nakba (الــنكبة), Arabic for "disaster", "catastrophe", or "cataclysm", also known as **the Palestinian Catastrophe**; marks the painful displacement of more than 700,000 Palestinian Arabs in 1948 when Israel was created by armed Zionist militias. Families were forced from their homes and land, losing everything whilst others were massacred [1]. Between 400 to 600 villages were destroyed, their Palestinian names erased and replaced with Hebrew ones. Today, **Nakba** stands as a symbol of resilience, reminding the world of Palestinian endurance amidst adversity and the ongoing struggle for justice, inspiring global solidarity. Despite the tragedy, Palestinians valiantly hold onto their heritage and dreams, determined to reclaim their rightful place and live in peace on their ancestral land. **The Nakba** is commemorated annually on May 15th, marking the day after the declaration of the State of Israel. Palestinians worldwide remember and honor the losses and displacement suffered during this period. Many organisations and communities around the world undertake educational initiatives aimed at fostering awareness about **the Nakba**, ensuring that younger generations comprehend the historical context and impact of this significant event. **Nakba** commemorations include cultural expressions such as art exhibitions, film screenings, and performances, serving as mediums to convey the collective memory and resilience of the Palestinian people.

[1] Read more about massacres and genocides under 'M' for "Massacres"

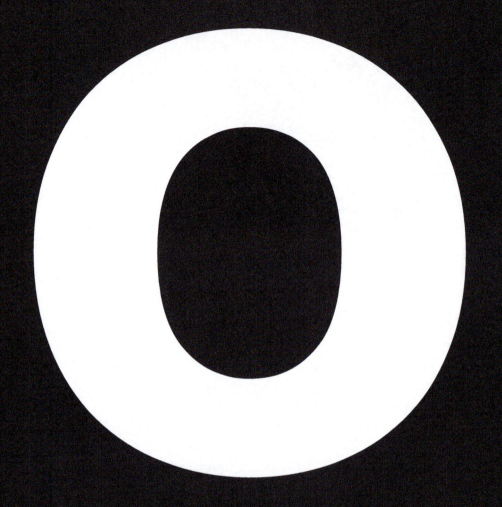

is for

Occupation

احتلال	
দখল	
Bezetting	
اشغال	
Occupation	
Besatzung	
कब्ज़ा	
Occupazione	
占領	
占领	
Okupacja	
Ocupação	
Оккупация	
Ocupación	
İşgal	
قبضہ	

The **occupation** of Palestine is a decades-long conflict rooted in history. In 1948, Israel was established on the usurped land of Palestinians, resulting in their displacement and exile to hundreds of thousands of Palestinians by armed Zionist militias. Israel's control has further extended to the West Bank, Gaza Strip, and East Jerusalem after the **1967 Six-Day War**. Today, around 2.8 million Palestinians live in the West Bank and 2.2 million people endure difficult conditions in Gaza as both face restrictions on movement and access to basic needs and resources, with Gaza in particular. The **occupation** of Palestine continues to impact millions of Palestinians. In the West Bank, Israeli settlements have expanded, leading to the continuous displacement of more and more Palestinian communities. Palestinians face restrictions on water, land access, and building permits, affecting their daily lives. In Gaza, a densely populated strip of land, the situation is dire. Unemployment rates hovers at around 50%, and the majority of the population relies on humanitarian aid. Additionally, frequent conflicts have left infrastructure severely damaged, making basic necessities like electricity and clean water scarce.

P

is for

Palestine

فلسطين

فلسطين

ফিলিস্তিন

Palestina

فلسطين

Palestine

Palästina

फ़िलिस्तीन

Palestina

パレスチナ

巴勒斯坦

Palestyna

Palestina

Палестина

Palestina

Filistin

فلسطين

Palestine, a land steeped in history and culture, bears witness to the enduring spirit of its people. For generations, Palestinians have called this ancient land home, cherishing its rich heritage. Their culture, woven with vibrant traditions, resonates in melodious music, captivating art, and a cuisine as diverse as their history. Palestinian culinary delights, from the aromatic flavours of **Falafel** and **Hummus** to the savoury goodness of **Maqluba** (a traditional rice dish), are a testament to their rich culinary heritage. Despite the challenges of occupation, Palestinians celebrate their identity through traditional dances like the **Dabke.** Historical cities like the capital city of **Jerusalem** and the city of **Bethlehem** resonate with centuries-old stories. **Jerusalem** holds religious significance for three major Abrahamic religions: Judaism, Christianity, and Islam. It is home to important religious sites, including the Western Wall, the Church of the Holy Sepulchre, and the Dome of the Rock. For Muslims, Jerusalem is the third holiest city and Palestinians see it as a symbol of their history and culture. The city's status is a key part of the Israel-Palestine issue, making it crucial for peace.

Q

is for

Al-Quds
(Jerusalem)

القدس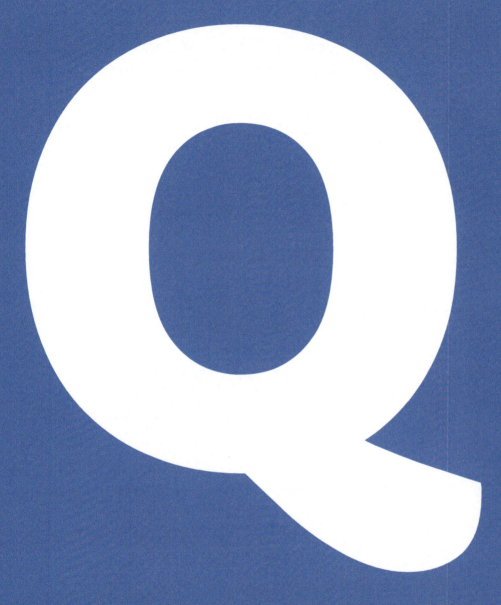

জেরুসালেম

Jeruzalem

اورشلیم

Jérusalem

Jerusalem

यरुशलेम

Gerusalemme

エルサレム

耶路撒冷

Jerozolima

Jerusalém

Иерусалим

Jerusalén

Kudüs

یروشلم

Al-Quds (الــقـدس), meaning "The Holy" in Arabic, holds profound significance as it symbolises Jerusalem — a city deeply cherished by Palestinians for its spiritual and historical importance. The ongoing struggle of the Palestinian people against Israeli occupation is intricately linked to Al-Quds, serving as a powerful embodiment of their resilience, cultural identity, and unwavering connection to the land. This city stands as a central focal point of Palestinian identity for a myriad of reasons:

(1) **Religious Significance:** Al-Quds is home to some of the holiest sites in Islam, including the Al-Aqsa Mosque (the third holiest site for Muslims), the Dome of the Rock, both revered by Muslims worldwide. The city also holds importance in Christianity and Judaism, making it a symbol of religious diversity such as and the Church of the Holy Sepulchre in Jerusalem, where many Christians believe Jesus was crucified, entombed, and resurrected. Israel's restrictions on Muslim access to **Al-Aqsa Mosque,** have repeatedly sparked tensions, with Muslims often need ing an Israeli permit for prayer and access. These restrictions contribute to ongoing concerns and disputes surrounding religious rights in the region.

(2) **Cultural Heritage:** Jerusalem has been a center of Palestinian culture for centuries. Its streets, markets, and landmarks are integral to the Palestinian narrative.

(3) **National Identity:** The struggle for control and sovereignty over Jerusalem is closely tied to the broader Palestinian struggle for self-determination.

(4) **Symbol of Resilience:** The ongoing challenges in and around Al-Quds, including the occupation and displacement, symbolise the resilience of the Palestinian people. Despite adversity, Palestinians continue to assert their connection to the city and their right to determine its future.

The status of Jerusalem remains a crucial aspect of any discussions surrounding a lasting and just resolution to the Palestinian issue.

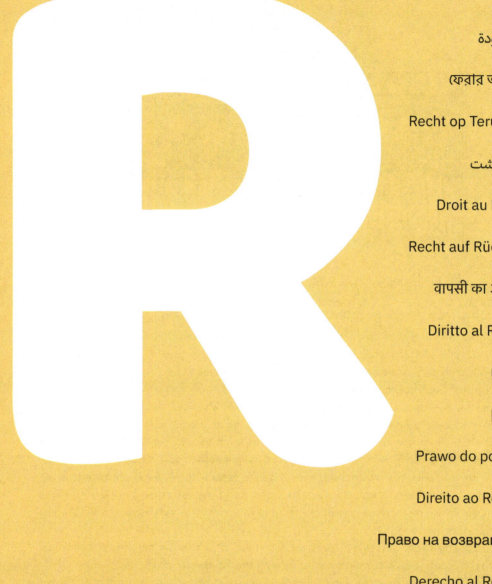

حق العودة

ফেরার অধিকার

Recht op Terugkeer

حق بازگشت

Droit au Retour

Recht auf Rückkehr

वापसी का अधिकार

Diritto al Ritorno

帰還権

回归权

Prawo do powrotu

Direito ao Retorno

Право на возвращение

Derecho al Retorno

Dönüş Hakkı

واپسی کا حق

is for
Right of
Return

Widely known as the **"Right of Return"**, it refers to the internationally recognised right of Palestinian refugees and their descendants to return to the homes and lands they were forced to leave during the conflict surrounding the creation of Israel in 1948. This right is based on UN General Assembly Resolution 194, which states that:

"refugees wishing to return to their homes and live at peace with their neighbours should be permitted to do so."

The Right of Return is a fundamental issue in the Palestinian struggle representing the Palestinians' demand for justice, recognition, and the restoration of their historical and property rights. It remains a central element in peace negotiations and continues to be a deeply significant and emotional issue for Palestinians, symbolising their enduring connection to their homeland.

The old-fashioned key is a symbol for the right of return, represents Palestinians' longing for their homes lost during **the Nakba** [1], when more than half of the population of Palestine were either expelled or fled violence in 1948. This yearning is passed through generations to this day, there are still many Palestinians who wear the keys to stolen homes around their necks for decades. The Arabic phrase **"We will return to Palestine"** (حـتماً سـنعود فلسـطين), is often used to express this determination despite displacement and occupation.

[1] Read more about the Nakba under 'N' for "The Nakba"

S

تضامن دولي

আন্তর্জাতিক সংহতি

Internationale Solidariteit

همبستگی بین‌المللی

Solidarité Internationale

Internationale Solidarität

अंतरराष्ट्रीय सामरस्य

Solidarietà Internazionale

国際連帯

国际团结

Międzynarodowa solidarność

Solidariedade Internacional

Международная солидарность

Solidaridad Internacional

Uluslararası Dayanışma

بین الاقوامی یکجہتی

is for

International
Solidarity

In the face of Israeli occupation, Palestinians find strength in **international solidarity**. Across continents, voices have risen up in unison, advocating for their rights, justice, and peace. **International solidarity** means nations, individuals, and organisations standing shoulder to shoulder with Palestine, condemning the injustices, and demanding lasting change. It's a global outcry against oppression, emphasising the shared humanity that unites us all. This solidarity manifests through rallies, humanitarian aid, boycotting campaigns and diplomatic efforts, creating a powerful force challenging the status quo, the occupying force, and and supporters of the occupation. Palestinians draw hope from this support, knowing they are not alone. Here are some examples of pro-Palestinian solidarity slogans and chants often used in demonstrations and protests:

"Free, free Palestine!"

"Justice for Palestine!"

"Palestinian lives matter!"

"End the siege, let Gaza live!"

"Occupation is a crime, free Palestine!"

"One, two, three, four, occupation no more,

Five, six, seven, eight, Israel is a terrorist state!"

"No justice, no peace! No occupation, release!"

"From Brooklyn to Gaza, occupation is a crime!"

"From the river to the sea, Palestine will be free!"

"Equal rights, end the fights, free, free Palestine!"

"Hey, hey, ho, ho, the occupation has got to go!"

"Resistance is justified when people are occupied!"

"Gaza, Gaza, don't you cry, Palestine will never die!"

"Boycott, divest, and sanction, until Palestine is free!"

"In our thousands, in our millions, we are all Palestinians!"

"Not another nickel, not another dime, no more money for Israel's crimes!"

T

is for

Thawra
Revolution (ثورة)

ثورة

বিপ্লব

Revolutie

انقلاب

Révolution

Revolution

क्रांति

Rivoluzione

革命

革命

Rewolucja

Revolução

Революция

Revolución

Devrim

انقلاب

"Thawra" (ثـــورة), a powerful Arabic term, embodies movements demanding transformative change. In Palestine's context, **Thawra** symbolises a seventy-five-year struggle against Israeli occupation, mirroring the enduring fight for justice. It transcends language, embodying the resilience of Palestinians facing injustice. **The Palestinian revolution** includes events such as the First Intifada (1987-1993) and the Second Intifada (2000-2005), which were marked by widespread protests, civil disobedience, and clashes with Israeli forces [1]. These periods were pivotal in mobilising global attention to the Palestinian cause and advocating for the recognition of Palestinian rights [2]. **Thawra** is more than a word; It expresses resistance and an unyielding call for justice. **Thawra** stands as a testament to the broader struggles for change, resonating with the spirit of movements like the Arab Spring, inspiring hope for a world where freedom triumphs over oppression and the dream of a just Palestine becomes a reality.

[1] Read more about uprisings in Palestine under 'U' for "Uprising (Intifada)"
[2] Read more about human right violations in Palestine under 'H' for "Human Rights"

U

انتفاضة

গণঅভ্যুত্থান / বিদ্রোহ

Opstand

انتفاضه

Soulèvement

Aufstand

विद्रोह

Insurrezione

反乱

起义

Powstanie (intifada)

Revolta

Восстание

Sublevación

Ayaklanma

انتفاضه

is for

Uprising
Intifada (انتفاضة)

Uprising, known as **Intifada** (انـتـفاضـة) in Arabic, symbolises the brave Palestinian spirit in the face of occupation. Intifada in Arabic literally means, "tremor", "shivering" or "shuddering". It is derived from the Arabic root word Nafada (نفض) i.e. "shake off" or "get rid of". Intifada is a grassroots movement, often led by youth, expressing frustration and demanding freedom. Fuelled by oppression, youth often resort to **stone-throwing** — another symbol of resistance in Palestine. **The First Intifada** began in 1987, a powerful protest against oppression, leading to international attention. **The Second Intifada** erupted in 2000 after peace talks stalled, causing significant unrest. These movements highlighted the resilience of Palestinians, amplifying their call for justice and self-determination. Despite challenges, Intifadas reflect the deep-rooted yearning for freedom, underscoring the ongoing struggle for Palestinian rights and a just resolution to the conflict.

is for

Victory
Sign

إشارة النصر

বিজয়ী চিহ্ন

Overwinningsgebaar

نشانه پیروزی

Signe de la Victoire

Siegeszeichen

विजयी संकेत

Segno della Vittoria

勝利のサイン

胜利手势

Znak zwycięstwa

Sinal da Vitória

Знак Победы

Señal de Victoria

Zafer İşareti

فتح کا نشان

56

The **victory sign** is a powerful gesture, where fingers form a "V" shape. For Palestinians, it embodies hope amid struggles. It's a symbol of their unwavering spirit, a testament to their resilience against adversity. Raised proudly, it signifies determination and the belief in a better tomorrow. Despite challenges, the **victory sign** became a beacon of optimism, uniting Palestinians and supporters alike, reminding them of their shared pursuit of peace, justice, and the triumph of human spirit over oppression. People and nations across the globe express solidarity with Palestine by raising the victory sign, which resonates globally, reflecting a shared commitment to Palestinian rights. From peaceful protests to social media campaigns, the **victory sign** unites voices worldwide, advocating for justice, freedom, and peace in Palestine.

W

is for

West Bank
الضفة الغربية

الضفة الغربية	
পশ্চিম তীর	
Westelijke Jordaanoever	
کرانه باختری	
Cisjordanie	
Westjordanland	
पश्चिमी तट	
Cisgiordania	
ヨルダン川西岸地区	
约旦河西岸	
Zachodni Brzeg Jordanu	
Cisjordânia	
Западный берег реки Иордан	
Cisjordania	
Batı Şeria	
مغربی ساحل	

The West Bank, a vital part of Palestine, is steeped in history and perseverance. Despite the ongoing Israeli occupation, Palestinians here continue their daily lives with remarkable resilience. Home to historic cities like Bethlehem and Hebron, it's a land dotted with ancient sites telling stories of centuries, such as (1) the ancient **city of Jericho**, considered one of the oldest inhabited cities in the world, and (2) **the Dead Sea**, Earth's lowest elevation on land. With over 2.8 million inhabitants, the West Bank faces ongoing challenges such as restricted movement and the growth of over 130 Israeli settlements, considered illegal under international law. These settlements encroach on Palestinian land, impacting livelihoods and fuelling tensions. Yet, amid adversity, Palestinians cultivate a vibrant culture, emphasising education and community.

X

is for

Xenophobia

كراهية الأجانب

অজ্ঞাতব্যক্তিভীতি ("জেনোফোবিয়া")

Xenofobie

کسوته‌گرایی

Xénophobie

Fremdenfeindlichkeit / Xenophobie

जर्मनवाद

Xenofobia

ゼノフォビア

仇外心理

Ksenofobia

Xenofobia

Ксенофобия

Xenofobia

Yabancı düşmanlığı / Ksenofobi

غیر ملکی کینہ

Xenophobia is defined as "the irrational fear, dislike, or prejudice against people from other countries or culture." The Palestinian people have faced historical injustices and displacement, and the conflict with the occupying forces often leads to tensions that can fuel xenophobic sentiments. Xenophobic behaviour towards Palestinians takes various forms and can indeed include deeply troubling actions such as humiliation and inflammatory rhetoric and chanting. Here are some examples:

(1) Hate Speech and Chants: Inflammatory slogans, including chants that express xenophobic sentiments, have been documented during protests and rallies in the occupied territories. Some incidents involve the chanting of slogans like *"Death to Arabs"*, *"Mohammed is Dead"*, *"A Good Arab is a Dead Arab"* *"May Your Village Burn Down"*, *"A Second Nakba is coming Soon"* and many more disturbing slogans; reflecting a disturbing manifestation of xenophobia.

(2) Anti-Arab Discrimination: Arab citizens of Israel face discrimination in various spheres, including employment and housing. Reports from human rights organisations highlight systemic issues that contribute to unequal treatment based on ethnicity.

(3) Checkpoints and Searches: Palestinians, whether residing in their homeland or in the diaspora, often face humiliating experiences at Israeli military checkpoints, where they may be subjected to rigorous searches and long delays. Such treatment can be degrading and impact the daily lives of Palestinians.

(4) Violence by Israeli Settlers: The UN reports a significant increase in violent incidents by Israeli settlers against Palestinians, which can range from physical assaults, intimidation and property damage to uprooting trees and poisoning livestock belonging to Palestinian farmers in the West Bank and on many occasions has led to the murder of innocent Palestinians.

(5) Media Stereotyping: Western and pro-Israeli media outlets often play a role in perpetuating stereotypes and presenting negative and false portrayals of Palestinians, thereby reinforcing biases and contributing to the creation of a hostile environment. This form of stereotyping undeniably exacerbates xenophobia and significantly influences public perceptions.

(6) Discriminatory Social Media Posts: Instances of xenophobic and discriminatory remarks against Palestinians have been observed on various social media platforms and in recent years has been on the rise.

(7) Legal Discrimination: Some discriminatory laws and policies impact Palestinians differently than Israeli citizens. For example, the Nation-State Law, passed in 2018, has been criticised for reinforcing the unequal status of non-Jewish citizens.

(8) Vandalism and Graffiti: Palestinian homes, mosques, and Christian sites have been targeted with vandalism and offensive graffiti. Such acts can include racist symbols and slogans.

(9) Attacks on Palestinian Workers: There have been reports of attacks on Palestinian workers in Israel, including incidents where workers were physically assaulted or verbally abused and in some instances killed.

(10) Violence Against African Asylum Seekers: While not directly related to the Palestinians, there have been instances of xenophobic violence against African asylum seekers in Israel, who were targeted based on their nationality, reflecting a broader problem of racism and xenophobia.

is for

Yearning
for Dignity

الشوق إلى الكرامة

মর্যাদার জন্য আকুল

Verlangen naar Waardigheid

آرزوی شان و کرامت

Aspiration à la Dignité

Sehnsucht nach Würde

गरिमा की आशा

Anelito alla Dignità

尊厳への渇望

对尊严的向往

Tęsknota za godnością

Anseio por Dignidade

Тоска по Достоинству

Anhelo por la Dignidad

Onur Arzusu

عزت کی خواہش

In Arabic, "Karama" (كـرامـة) translates to mean "**dignity**". It represents the quality of being worthy of honor and respect as a human being. In the context of the Palestinian struggle, **"Karama"** embodies the fundamental human right to live with dignity, free from oppression, inequality and non-discrimination. **Yearning for Dignity** is the heartbeat of Palestine's struggle. It's the fierce pride that keeps Palestinians standing tall amid occupation's challenges. Despite hardships, they assert their worth, demanding respect and equality. **Dignity** is their unyielding spirit, the light that guides them through dark times. In the face of adversity, it fuels their resilience, echoing their call for justice worldwide. It's not just a word; it's their essence, their unshakable belief in their own humanity. Palestinians, in their pursuit of dignity, inspire the world with their strength, reminding us all of the universal right to live with honor and respect.

is for

Zionism

الصهيونية	🇵🇸
সিয়োনবাদ / জায়নবাদ	🇧🇩
Zionisme	🇳🇱
صهیونیسم	☬
Sionisme	🇫🇷
Zionismus	🇩🇪
ज़ायनिज़्म	🇮🇳
Sionismo	🇮🇹
シオニズム	🇯🇵
锡安主义	🇨🇳
Syjonizm	🇵🇱
Sionismo	🇵🇹
Сионизм	🇷🇺
Sionismo	🇪🇸
Siyonizm	🇹🇷
صهیونیزم	🇵🇰

Zionism, is the political ideology whose main aim is to establish a homeland for Jews in the Middle East, however, this carries another layer - a narrative of unfair occupation and oppression for Palestinians. It's a story of conflicting dreams, where one's aspiration becomes another's struggle for dignity. For Palestinians, **Zionism** signifies a challenging chapter, marked by displacement, injustice and oppression. Yet, in the face of this adversity, Palestinians stand resilient. Their narrative weaves a tale of resistance against oppression, echoing the spirit of endurance and hope. The dangers of unchecked **Zionism** lie in the expansion of Israeli settlements, leading to land confiscation and the oppressive limiting of resources to Palestinians. Additionally, it has created significant obstacles to peace, perpetuating a cycle of tension and conflict in the region. The struggle against these challenges forms an integral part of the Palestinian narrative, highlighting the need for a just and lasting resolution to the Israeli occupation of Palestine.

An ABC of
Solidarity
with
Palestine

An A to Z Guide to
Advocacy and Action

A Advocate

Speak up for the rights and justice of Palestinians in your conversations at home, work, social media, and within your community. Engage in conversations with friends and family to share information, foster understanding, and dispel misconceptions about what is and has happened in Palestine.

B Boycott

Refuse to purchase goods and services from companies that contribute to the financing of arms in Israel. Consider supporting the Boycott, Divestment, and Sanctions (BDS) movement as a means to pressure entities contributing to the occupation.

C Collaborate

Engage in partnerships with individuals and organisations committed to Palestinian rights, actively participating in campaigns and initiatives that promote awareness, freedom, and the cessation of oppression.

D Demonstrate

Engage in peaceful protests, vigils and demonstrations to visibly express solidarity with Palestinians. Rally your friends and family to join you in advocating for justice, raising awareness about Palestine, and pushing for positive change.

E Educate

Stay informed about the historical and current context of the Palestinian issue. Educate yourself and inform others within your close network. Create and share educational content via your communication channels to foster a deeper understanding about the rights of Palestinians.

F Fundraise & Donate

Organise or participate in fundraising activities to support charitable initiatives benefiting Palestinians. Donate to reputable organisations working on humanitarian aid, education, and development in the occupied land of Palestine.

G Grassroots Activism

Get involved in local grassroots movements and organisations advocating for Palestinian rights.

H Humanitarian Support

Support organisations providing all kinds of humanitarian aid such as medical, food, shelter and other essential resources to those affected by conflict.

I Interfaith Engagement

Foster understanding and collaboration through interfaith dialogue, promoting unity among diverse communities.

J Join

Join efforts for justice by actively engaging in local initiatives. Join like-minded individuals to amplify your collective impact, working collaboratively to advocate for the rights of Palestinians and foster positive change in the Israeli-Palestinian conflict.

K Knowledge Sharing

Share informative articles, documentaries, and books about the Palestinian cause to raise awareness.

L Letters to Representatives

Write letters to your government representatives urging them to address the humanitarian and political aspects of the conflict. Urge them to call for an immediate ceasefire in Gaza (2023)

M Media Literacy

Be critical of misleading, false or biased media narratives, seek diverse sources, and encourage accurate reporting on the Palestinian issue.

N	**Network**	Connect and network with local and international organisations working towards justice and equality for Palestinians.
O	**Organise Events**	Plan, participate and organise awareness-raising events, such as talks, webinars, or cultural activities.
P	**Promote Palestine**	Counter misinformation by promoting and celebrating Palestinian culture and history. Share authentic narratives, traditions, and achievements, to dispel misconceptions surrounding the rich cultural heritage of the Palestinian people.
Q	**Question Bias**	Challenge biased narratives and stereotypes, in conversations and in the media, promoting fair and accurate representations of Palestinians.
R	**Refugee Support**	Assist organisations working with Palestinian refugees, who face unique challenges and hardships. Notable organisations include UNRWA, UNICEF, PCRF, MAP, and many others.
S	**Support Student Initiatives**	Encourage student-led initiatives on university campuses, by organising events, scholarly dialogues, lectures and conferences, and awareness campaigns to foster understanding and support for Palestine.
T	**Trade Ethically**	Promote conscientious consumer choices by supporting businesses and products that adhere to principles of justice and human rights. Consider purchasing from Palestinian traders in the West Bank, avoiding those with ties to the occupation or involved in human rights

U — Use Social Media

Harness the power of social media to share authentic information, increase awareness, and rally support for the Palestinian cause. Blog and share personal stories, utilise hashtags strategically, and participate in online petitions and campaigns.

V — Volunteer

Contribute your time and skills to organisations dedicated to Palestinian rights and humanitarian efforts.

W — Wear Solidarity Symbols

Wear or display symbols to spark conversations and visually express your support for the Palestinian cause. Key symbols include: the Palestinian flag, the *Kuffiyah*, the key of "The Right of Return", *Handala*, the olive tree, and many others.

X — Xenophobia Awareness

Raise awareness on the harm of xenophobia to Palestinians, advocate for inclusivity, and foster empathy. Strive for an inclusive environment respecting the rights and dignity of all, regardless of background.

Y — Youth Engagement

Inspire the youth to educate themselves about the Palestinian issue and join open discussions. Empower them to be informed advocates, fostering a generation committed to justice and positive change.

Z — Zero Tolerance for Injustice

Advocate for a zero-tolerance stance on injustice, urging individuals and organisations to condemn human rights violations in Palestine.

Acknowledgments

I would like to express my gratitude to my colleagues and my students at the University of Edinburgh and beyond for their generous and valuable suggestions, corrections, support and encouragement in this venture. I am indebted specifically to the following people for their review of the manuscript and support with the multilingual translations. Any shortcomings remaining in the book are my responsibility.

Mr. Haitham Awaad

Diana Meirinho Domingues, University of Edinburgh

Dr Kholoud al-Ajarma, Alwaleed Centre for the Study of Islam in the Contemporary World, U. Of Edinburgh

Dr. Montasir Fayez Faris Al Hamad, University of Qatar

Linn Pfitzner, University of Edinburgh

Fumiko Narumi-Munro, University of Edinburgh

Aldona Judina, University of Edinburgh

Dr. Anthony Gorman, University of Edinburgh

Dr. Azin Mostajer Haghighi, University of Edinburgh

Dr. Mark McLeister, University of Edinburgh

Anthony Till, Manchester Metropolitan University

Dr Carmen Herrero, Manchester Metropolitan University

Dr. Jehan Al-Azzawi, Edinburgh City Council

Rania Alabbadi, University of Edinburgh

Liwen Chen, University of Edinburgh

Astrid Chen, University of Edinburgh

Rania Alabbadi, University of Edinburgh

Ozge Ozsaylan, University of Edinburgh

Kushagra Goyal, University of Edinburgh

Alvaro Muniz Brea, University of Edinburgh

Zoey van Hest, University of Edinburgh

Dua Zaid

Iyad Sawaftah

Piotr Talarczyk

Final Words

I hope you found this book both enjoyable and insightful. Your reflections on the ways in which you've benefited from it would be immensely valuable. If you have any questions or would like to share your thoughts, please feel free to reach out to me at m.diouri@me.com. You can also connect with me on Twitter/X: @e_Arabic or visit my website at mouradd.com. I look forward to hearing from you.

Mourad Diouri
Edinburgh, Scotland
26 Oct 2023

About the Author

Mourad Diouri is an author and teaching fellow of Arabic at the University of Edinburgh in Scotland, UK. In addition to writing instructional books on learning Arabic as a foreign language, he also works as an education consultant, external examiner and teacher trainer within the UK and internationally. He lives in Edinburgh, Scotland, with his wife and children.

Also by Mourad Diouri

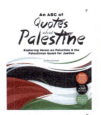 An ABC of Quotes About Palestine: Exploring Voices on Palestine & the Palestinian Quest for Justice (2023)

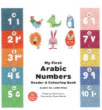 My First Arabic Numbers Reader & Colouring Book, Mosaic Tree Press (2023)

 An Abc of Palestine: A Journey To Discover Palestine & The Palestinian People For Kids & Grown Ups (2023)

 My First Arabic Colours: Reader & Activity Book for Kids, Mosaic Tree Press (2023)

 My Journey Through The Most Beautiful Names of Allah: Arabic Reader & Activity Book for Kids: **(Volume 1, 2 & 3)** (2023)

 My Arabic Learning Journals: My Abc Dictionary (English-Arabic), Mosaic Tree Press (2022)

 My First Arabic Alphabet & Colouring Book [Arabic for Little Ones] (2023)

 My Arabic Learning Journals: My Abc Dictionary (Arabic- English), Mosaic Tree Press (2022)

 My Arabic Animal Alphabet Reader, Arabic for Little Ones, Mosaic Tree Press (2023)

 My Arabic Learning Journals: Thematic Vocabulary, Mosaic Tree Press (2022)

 My First Arabic Alphabet Reader, Arabic for Little Ones, Mosaic Tree Press (2023)

 Tricky Tongue Twisters In Arabic (Arabic Script & Sounds),[Essential Arabic Readers] (2023)

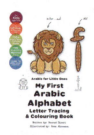

My First Arabic Alphabet: Letter Tracing & Colouring Book [Arabic for Little Ones] (2023)

I Am .... An ABC of Empowering Self-Affirmations: A Guided Journal for Self-Discovery, Self-Growth & Resilience (2022)

Essential Arabic Readers: Alphabet Letters with Vowels & Pronunciation Symbols, Mosaic Tree Press (2022)

My Journey through Ramadan & Eid Al-Fitr (Arabic for Little Ones), Mosaic Tree Press (2023)

Similar Sounding Letters in Arabic: Essential Arabic Readers (2023)

CoronaVirus Lexicon: A Practical Guide for Arabic Learners & Translators (M. Diouri & M. Aboelezz 2023)

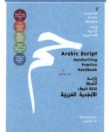

Essential Arabic Readers: Arabic Alphabet Writing Practice Handbook, Mosaic Tree Press (2023)

Teach Yourself: Essential Arabic Vocabulary: A Handbook of Core Terms, Hodder Education (2015)

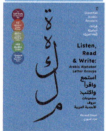

Listen, Read & Write: Arabic Alphabet Letter Groups [Essential Arabic Readers] (2023)

Internet Arabic: Essential Middle Eastern Vocabularies (w/ MP3 CD), Edinburgh University Press (2013)

Arabic & Islamic Mosaic & Calligraphy Colouring Journal (Volume 1: Islamic Quotes) (2022)

Teach Yourself: Read & Write Arabic Script, Hodder Education (2011)

Browse our full catalogue at

MosaicTree.org

 Arabic Script & Sounds

 Arabic Vocabulary

 Arabic for Little Ones

 Arabic/Islamic Mosaic & Calligraphy

 Arabic Learning Journals

 Well-Being & Character Development

MosaicTree.org

Completed with the grace of God

Printed in Great Britain
by Amazon